Anne Frank's Story

Anne Frank's Story

Her life retold
for children

Carol Ann Lee

First U.S. edition published in 2002.

Text copyright © 2001 by Carol Ann Lee.
Introduction copyright © 2001 by Diane Louise Jordan.
Map copyright © Venture Graphics.
Photographs copyright © AFF/AFS/Archive Photos.

All quotations from Anne Frank's Diary *are under copyright of the Anne Frank-Fonds, Basel, Switzerland. The letters of the Frank family and Otto Frank's memoir are used by kind permission of Buddy Elias. The text of the pen-pal letter and Anne's verse in her friend's poetry album are reproduced courtesy of the Simon Wiesenthal Center, Los Angeles.*

Published by Troll Communications L.L.C.

Reprinted by arrangement with Jane Judd, Puffin Books, and RLR Associates, Ltd.

Printed in Canada.

10 9 8 7 6 5 4 3 2

Library of Congress Cataloging-in-Publication Data

Lee, Carol Ann.
   Anne Frank's story / Carol Ann Lee.
      p. cm.
   Summary: Expands on the story of Anne Frank revealed in her diary by providing
details about the family and friends who shaped her life and gave her the strength to
endure two years of hiding in an attic in Nazi-occupied Holland.
      ISBN 0-8167-7427-7
      1. Frank, Anne, 1929–1945—Juvenile literature.   2. Holocaust, Jewish
(1939–1945)—Netherlands—Amsterdam—Juvenile literature.   3. Jews—
Netherlands—Amsterdam—Biography—Juvenile literature.   4. Jewish children in the
Holocaust—Netherlands—Amsterdam—Biography—Juvenile literature.   5. Amsterdam
(Netherlands)—Biography—Juvenile literature.   [1. Frank, Anne, 1929–1945.
2. Jews—Netherlands—Biography.   3. Holocaust, Jewish (1939–1945)—Netherlands—
Amsterdam.   4. Women—Biography.]   I. Title.
DS135.N6 F7339   2002
940.53'18'092—dc21
   [B]   2001054836

For River Jake

Contents

Map of Europe in January 1939

NORTH SEA

DENMARK
Copenh

Westerbork

Amsterdam
THE NETHERLANDS

London

Bergen-Belsen

Elbe

Ber

GERMA

English Channel

BELGIUM

Brussels

Aachen

Rhine

Frankfurt-am-Main

LUXEMBOURG
Luxembourg

Paris

Meuse

FRANCE

Danube

Basel

AUS

SWITZERLAND

Lyon

Milan

Rhône

ITALY

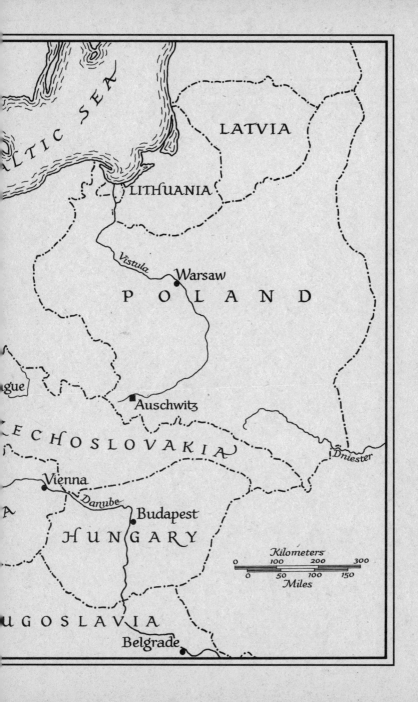

Editor's Note

Readers may notice that some of the names in this book are different from those in Anne Frank's diary. The author of this book has used the real names of each person who hid in the Secret Annexe and each person who helped them.

When Otto Frank, Anne's father, first published her diary, he decided to use the fictional names Anne had created for some of their friends. Mr. Frank changed the van Pels family name to van Daan and Fritz Pfeffer became Albert Dussel. Mr. Frank also changed the names of some of his staff. Mr. Kugler was changed to Mr. Kraler, Mr. Kleiman became Mr. Koophuis, and Bep Voskuijl became Elli Vossen.

Preface

"Here is your daughter's legacy to you."

These were the words of Miep Santrouschitz, Austrian-born secretary to Otto Frank.

It was the summer of 1945. War in Europe was finally over, leaving in its wake a trail of destroyed countries, homes, families, and lives.

Miep placed a red-checked journal into Otto's hands. She was right, but not only was Anne's diary Otto Frank's legacy— it and Anne's story have become a rich inheritance for the world.

Like many others before me, I have read Anne's diary and have marveled at a young person, wise beyond her years, whose ability to use the written word to convey her innermost thoughts and feelings has captivated us all.

The following pages allow us to get to know Anne even more. We discover details about her family and friends, the places she called home, and the way that she lived. We see the backdrop of her short life unfold and can be forgiven at times for thinking that Anne was just an ordinary girl growing up within an ordinary, secure, and loving family. In fact, the Franks were quite an *extraordinary* family, and we learn of how often they rose above unthinkable discrimination to make the best of every situation.

Anne Frank's Story allows *us* to experience her life and to watch this "normal, lively child" growing up, from her early days in Frankfurt, where she was born in 1929, through to her untimely death at Bergen-Belsen concentration camp in 1945.

Despite the growing power of anti-Jewish feeling in Europe, Otto and Edith Frank worked hard to protect their daughters' interests and to enable them to grow up having fun and as much freedom as possible. They show us all how important it is to protect and jealously guard our family life.

Anne and her sister, Margot, courageously demonstrate the incredible ability children have to enjoy their childhood in spite of appalling hardships. We are clearly reminded of the importance of friends and relationships and how loyalty is one of the greatest gifts we can give to those we love.

As we stand in the dawn of a new millennium, I would love to believe that the world has learned—has moved on from the terrible persecution reported in these pages. I would love to believe that childhood is sacred and remains untouched by hatred and discrimination. I would love to believe that such horror will never again be witnessed or experienced by young or old alike.

Sadly, even recent history has shown that my belief is in vain. However, I cling on to hope. Hope that those of us who read *Anne Frank's Story* or Anne's diary, or who know of her life, will find her an inspiration and will continue to strive for the ideals for which she continued to strive.

Diane Louise Jordan
British TV and Radio Presenter and
friend of The Anne Frank Trust

Anne Frank's
Story

Introduction: Europe at the Time of Anne Frank

The Nazi Party was already on its rise to power in Germany in 1929 when Anne Frank was born. The party, led by Adolf Hitler, believed that certain groups of people —Jews, black people, Jehovah's Witnesses, Gypsies, the physically and mentally handicapped, homosexuals— had no right to live in ordinary society. Above all, they hated the Jews (this is called anti-Semitism; people who dislike Jews are anti-Semites). Hitler often gave speeches in which he said that Jews were lazy, greedy people who were ruining the country. But in fact, many German Jews had valuable, useful jobs; they were teachers, doctors, lawyers, bankers, and shopkeepers. Thousands of Jewish men had fought for Germany in World War I. Many people believed Hitler, however, because Germany was going through a difficult time economically (having lost badly in the First World War), and they needed to blame someone for their problems. Hitler promised the German people a brighter future—which he said would come about once there were no more Jews in the country.

In 1933, Hitler and the Nazis gained absolute power in the German parliament, called the *Reichstag*. From then on, anyone who opposed the Nazis' laws was beaten, imprisoned, and often murdered. There were many attacks on minority groups, and on the Jews in particular. Two special groups of Nazi police were placed in control of German society: the Gestapo (the police force) and the SS (an elite army corps). Jews in Germany lost their jobs and all their rights as German citizens. Some began to leave the country. Many families sent their children away to safety in England via a specially organized operation called the *Kindertransporte*—the children's transport. Some families were split apart, often forever.

On September 15, 1935, the *Reichstag* passed two new laws to "protect German blood and German honor." This meant that Jews could no longer call themselves German, fly the German flag, employ a German woman as domestic help, or go out with or marry Aryans (the name given to white, non-Jewish Germans). With a growing sense of doom, more than 50,000 Jewish people left Germany for other countries, where they believed they would be safe.

On March 12, 1938, Austria was invaded by German troops and became part of Nazi Germany. Austrian Jews immediately suffered under the very harsh new laws that the Nazis imposed. Later that year, a young Jewish student killed a high-ranking officer in the Nazi Party. The Nazis used this as an excuse to attack Jewish communities throughout Germany. On November 9 and 10, 1938, thousands of Jewish men were sent to concentration camps, where they were made to work as prisoners, under terrible conditions; synagogues were set on fire; hundreds of Jewish books were burned; and Jewish shop windows were broken. These horrifying events became known as *"Kristallnacht"* which means "Night of the Broken Glass," after the shattered glass lying on the pavement.

On September 1, 1939, German troops invaded Poland, and as a result, two days later France and Britain declared war on Germany. World War II had begun. As country after country was invaded by the German army, Jews everywhere began to fear for their lives. The Frank family, living in the Netherlands, was among those caught in the Nazi net when the country was occupied by Germany in May 1940. What had already happened in Germany now began happening in the Netherlands: month by month, Jews were told they could not visit certain places or do certain things, and their jobs were taken from them. In theaters, cafés, restaurants, and parks, signs began to appear, warning Jews that they were unwelcome. After April 29, 1942, all Jews above the age of six in the Netherlands had to wear a special badge. This was a big six-pointed star on yellow fabric with the word "*Jood*" (Jew) on it. Many other new laws were put into effect at the same time, so that no one was quite sure what was forbidden and what was not. Then, in July 1942, the Germans began regularly deporting Jews by the thousands from all over Europe to the concentration camps. The deportations continued throughout 1943 and 1944. From the Netherlands alone, 12,000 Jews a month were put on special trains that took them to concentration camps and almost certainly to their deaths.

When the war ended in 1945, the first shocking pictures of the survivors of these terrible concentration camps were published in newspapers, and special documentary films were shown in theaters. Some people could not believe the horrors that they saw, and others could not bring themselves to look. There are still people, even today, who believe that the Holocaust never happened. But it did, and 6 million people were killed. From the Netherlands alone, 110,000 Jews were deported; only 5,000 returned.

Anne Frank was not among them.

Chapter One:
From Frankfurt to Amsterdam

"I want to see something of the world and do all
kinds of exciting things!"
(*Anne Frank's Diary*, May 8, 1944)

Many people kept diaries during the last century, but the
most famous diary writer of them all is a young Jewish
girl named Anne Frank. Anne began writing in her diary
at the age of thirteen, and she wrote in it almost every
day for the next two years. At first, she told Kitty—the
name she gave the diary—about her friends, school, and
boys, but very soon she could no longer write about
these things. It was 1942, and the middle of the Second
World War, a time of fear and uncertainty, especially for
Jewish families in Europe. Anne and her parents and
sister were forced to go into hiding to escape being sent
away from Amsterdam, the city in which they had lived
for almost ten years. The Netherlands, along with many
other European countries, was occupied by the German
army, and concentration camps—where Jews were

worked, starved, and put to death—had been set up all over Europe. Anne eventually died in one of these camps, just before her sixteenth birthday, but the lively, mischievous girl, who had been nicknamed "The Chatterbox" by her teachers, left behind one of the most powerful documents ever written: her diary.

No one, least of all Anne's own family and friends, could have guessed that her words would become so famous, although it was clear to everyone right from the start that Anne Frank had a lot to say about everything. She was born on June 12, 1929, in Frankfurt-am-Main, a German city, where her relatives had lived for over four centuries. Anne's parents, Otto and Edith Frank, already had one daughter, Margot Betti, who was three years older than Anne. Margot was gentle and kind, and she was very happy to have a new little sister. The baby already had a mass of dark hair, and she soon showed an interest in the world around her. When Anne was old enough to stand, her mother placed her crib on the balcony of their house on Marbachweg so that the curious little girl could gaze at the streets and people passing by.

Anne was as friendly as Margot was shy; they were already classic cases of the sensible, quiet older sister and the high-spirited, noisy younger one. Margot was always clean and neat, a "little princess," while Anne enjoyed getting into mischief, sitting in puddles, and making her clothes dirty. If Anne was not watched with a careful eye, anything could happen! But Anne and Margot shared one similarity: they both adored their father, who had endless patience and a good sense of humor. He liked to tell his daughters stories about two sisters, not unlike themselves: Bad Paula and Good Paula. Margot knew that she liked Good Paula best, but Anne never quite managed to pick a favorite. Later on, when the family had to go into hiding, Anne's father would keep her calm with new stories about the two Paulas.

Anne's early life in Frankfurt was very happy; two slightly older cousins, Stephan and Buddy, lived nearby and would visit often, and the girls were sometimes taken to their grandmother's house, where they all played together. One outing almost ended in disaster, as Buddy recalls: "My brother and I took Anne outside in her pram [baby carriage]. We went racing around and around the street, but we couldn't get the curb right and the pram tipped up. Anne flew out of the pram! We told no one of course, and Anne was okay."[1] It was safer when Stephan stuck to his impression of Charlie

---

[1] Elias, Buddy, author interview, Cheltenham, October 1997.

Chaplin, which was a great favorite with Anne and Margot.

In March 1931, when Anne was almost two years old, the Frank family had to leave their apartment on Marbachweg. The Nazi Party, an extreme political group led by Adolf Hitler, was growing more powerful and gaining more supporters; the owner of the Franks' apartment was a Nazi, and he did not want Jews living in his house. The family found a new home on Ganghoferstrasse, not far away. It was smaller inside but had a yard and large garden, ideal for Anne and Margot to play in. Opposite the house was an overgrown field, and close by there were hills, perfect for tobogganing when it snowed. This particularly appealed to Margot, who had a sleigh in which to pull her baby sister around.

At first, Anne was too young to go outside the garden, and she played instead in the sandbox or, on very hot days, in a big old metal tub filled with water. There were plenty of other children in the neighborhood too, and there would often be a noisy group of them having fun. Some of these friends were not Jewish, and this gave Anne and Margot a chance to learn about other religions, which their parents encouraged. Otto and Edith Frank were not very religious at all. They were more concerned about their daughters' education, which they believed was very important. As Margot and Anne grew older, they began to read from their father's collection of books. Margot tended to keep her thoughts and opinions to herself, but when Anne learned to talk she was just the opposite, and whatever popped into her mind also popped out of her mouth. As a three-year-old she once surprised everyone at her friend Gertrud Naumann's home, when she fixed her gaze on Gertrud's father and exclaimed, "Why, you have eyes exactly like a cat!"[2]

Otto Frank loved to take photographs of his young family, and there are many pictures of Anne and Margot with their friends, at parties, and at home posing in front of mirrors or pretending to brush their teeth. The last photograph he took of them in Frankfurt shows Anne and Margot with their mother in the city center, all bundled up in warm coats. It was March 1933. Although they had enjoyed their day out, on their walk home they had noticed a frightening new form of graffiti: vicious anti-Jewish slogans on the doors and windows of Jewish-owned shops.

When she was born, Anne was given a silver necklace

---

[2] Schnabel, Ernst, *The Footsteps of Anne Frank*, Pan Books, London, 1976, p. 21.

on which hung a triangle with the words "Lucky Charm, 12.6.1929, Frankfurt-am-Main." Anne, like thousands of other Jewish children in Germany at that time, needed all the luck in the world: the Nazis believed that every Jew had to be destroyed. The days of freedom, weekends in Aachen visiting Anne's grandmother, and trips to local beauty spots were coming to an end. A new law stated that Jewish children could not attend the same schools as non-Jews. Anne was due to start nursery school in September 1933, but as a Jewish child, she was no longer welcome. Margot would have to leave the school she loved, and where she was proving herself to be an excellent student, and find another. In the center of Frankfurt, where the Nazis had just been elected to the local council, there was a demonstration on the steps of the town hall. Uniformed Nazis raised their arms in salute to their leader, Adolf Hitler, and screamed, "Jews out! Jews out!" The red-white-and-black Party flag with its hooked cross, the swastika, was unfurled across the building. The chanting continued, and supporters on the streets joined in. Otto and Edith Frank knew that the time had come for them to leave, before it was too late.

The Frank family was among 63,000 Jews who left Germany in 1933. Other relatives had already fled the country or were preparing to flee. Anne's uncle Herbert moved to Paris, and her uncle Robert settled in London with his wife. Grandmother Frank and Anne's cousins Stephan and Buddy, together with their parents, had already left Germany to live in Switzerland. There was nothing to keep the Franks in Germany, particularly since Otto Frank's bank business had finally closed down. Stephan and Buddy's father, Erich Elias, had opened a branch of the company Opekta in Switzerland. Opekta produced pectin, a substance used in jam-making, and was doing very well. Erich Elias asked Otto Frank whether he would be interested in setting up another branch of Opekta in the Netherlands. Mr. Frank liked the idea, and so he left Germany in June 1933 to find a suitable home for his family. Meanwhile, Mrs. Frank, Margot, and Anne moved to Aachen, where they lived with Grandmother Hollander, Mrs. Frank's mother.

In Amsterdam, Anne's father worked hard to make sure that his new business was a success. Among his staff were Miep Santrouschitz and Victor Kugler. Miep was a young Austrian-born woman. At Opekta, Miep learned how to make jam before taking charge of the typing, the bookkeeping, and the "Complaint and Information" desk, where she dealt with customers' problems and inquiries. Kugler, also an Austrian, supervised all the employees. He was a very serious man but kind and straightforward. Miep and Kugler quickly became close friends with Anne's father; one day they would save his life.

Otto Frank was desperately lonely for his wife and daughters and spent every spare minute looking for a suitable home for them. He had taken rooms on the second floor of an apartment block at Stadionkade 24, a short tram ride from Amsterdam's center, but his search took him to Nieuwe Amsterdam-Zuid, where Miep lived. There he found the perfect family apartment.

Mrs. Frank and Margot boarded a train for the Netherlands on December 5, 1933. Anne remained with her grandmother in Aachen until February 1934, when she was "put on Margot's table as a birthday present."[3] She was not quite five years old. Her mother wrote to a friend, "Both children are full of fun. Anne a little comedian."[4]

---

[3] *Anne Frank's Diary*, June 15, 1942. Margot Frank turned eight years old in February 1934—hence Anne's reference to being her birthday present.
[4] Frank, Edith, letter, March 1934, in Schnabel, Ernst, *The Footsteps of Anne Frank*, Pan Books, London, 1976, p. 25.

Chapter Two:
Carefree School Days

"When we were still part of ordinary, everyday life,
everything was just marvelous. ..."
(From "Do You Remember?")[1]

Many Jewish refugees from Nazi Germany settled in
south Amsterdam. The Frank family lived in the area
called the River Quarter. On one side was the River
Amstel with its painted barges, and there were lots of
bakeries and coffee shops in the neighborhood. The smell
of warm bagels drifted in the air, and pickle shops had
carts outside on which was written: "The Best Pickles in
Amsterdam!" Small cafés were always packed with
gossiping men and women. The Franks' new apartment
at 37 Merwedeplein overlooked a grassy square to the
front and gardens and other houses to the back.

Anne's and Margot's schools were only five minutes'
walk away from their home. Sometimes Anne was

---

[1] Frank, Anne, "Do You Remember?" July 7, 1943, in *Tales from the Secret Annexe*,
Penguin, London, 1982, p. 93.

accompanied by her teacher, Mr. van Gelder, on her morning stroll to school. She liked to chat with him and repeated the stories and poems she and her father made up together. At school, Anne was always with her two best friends, Hanneli Goslar and Sanne Ledermann. People nicknamed them Anne, Hanne, and Sanne. Hanneli (also known as Lies) and Sanne were from Germany originally too, and they had all arrived in the Netherlands about the same time as the Frank family. Lies and Anne were especially good friends; Lies lived on the same street, in an apartment just below the Franks'.

The girls all played together after school. They loved hopscotch, and performing cartwheels and doing handstands against walls. Anne was hopeless at cartwheels and handstands, but she tried her best. The girls kept poetry albums too, along with all the other children in the neighborhood. Friends wrote short verses to each other and illustrated them. During school vacations and on weekends, children called for each other by whistling their signature tunes through the mail slot. To her great disappointment, Anne could not whistle. She sang instead—five notes up, five notes down —everyone knew when Anne was there!

Mr. Frank, Margot, and Anne soon learned to speak

Dutch. Mrs. Frank found the language more difficult and missed their old home in Germany a great deal. But there was always something pleasant happening. In 1934 the family went to stay with Grandma, who still lived in Aachen, and took day trips to the seaside. On June 12 of that year, Anne celebrated her fifth birthday with a party at home.

Schoolwork proved a slight problem for Anne because she disliked having to sit still for too long. Margot was one of the best pupils at her school and already talked about going on to college. Like everyone else, their father could see quite clearly the differences between his daughters: "Anne was always popular with boys and girls . . . a normal, lively child who delighted us and frequently upset us. Whenever she entered a room, there was a fuss. . . . Margot was the bright one. Everybody admired her. She got along with everybody."[2]

Anne also found school a chore because she was often ill. She had contracted rheumatic fever and had a weak heart. Her arms and legs would frequently dislocate as well, a source of much amusement to Anne herself, who thought it hilarious to crack her shoulder in and out of

---

[2] Frank, Otto, "Anne was always . . ." in Farrell, E. C., "Postscript to a Diary," *The Global Magazine*, March 6, 1965; "a normal, lively . . ." in "The Living Legacy of Anne Frank," *Journal*, September 1967; "Margot was . . ." in article by Straus, R. Peter, *Moment*, December 1977.

its socket before horrified friends. She had to rest every afternoon and could not play any demanding sports, but she took lessons in rhythmic gymnastics, which she enjoyed, and learned to swim and ice-skate as well. Margot was not a strong girl either, and often suffered from stomachaches. The family's summer vacation of 1935 was divided between the beach and their relatives' villa, where both sisters benefited from the fresh air and sun.

Despite the troubles in Germany and elsewhere, in Amsterdam Anne and Margot could still enjoy their childhood. Family members came to stay, and there were visits to Switzerland, where their cousins lived. Just as Anne and Lies had become close friends, so too did their parents. The Goslars were religious and practiced all aspects of their Jewish faith. The Franks were not as religious, though Edith Frank became very involved with the Liberal Jewish synagogue, whose rules were not so strict. Otto Frank rarely attended, and of the two girls, Margot was clearly the more interested in religion. The Franks usually spent Friday night, the start of the Jewish Sabbath, at the Goslars' house, and they celebrated the Jewish festival of Passover together. They also celebrated Christmas, which Lies's parents did not, although Lies was allowed to join in the school party and the Franks' festivities. Both families were always together on New Year's Eve.

On Wednesday afternoons and Sunday mornings, Lies studied Hebrew. Margot also took classes, but Anne preferred to spend Sundays with her father at his office. Lies joined her in the afternoons, and they pretended to be secretaries, calling each other on the office telephones and getting into mischief. Their favorite trick was throwing cups of cold water down onto passersby. Lies did not attend school on Saturday, since it was the Jewish Sabbath, but went to synagogue in the morning with a girl from Margot's school. Anne was jealous of the friendship and later wrote about it in her diary. Lies and Anne were very close during this time, however. They confided their secrets, teased each other, traded postcards of the British and Dutch royal families, shared the same dentist, called for each other with their special tune, and even, in 1936, caught a number of illnesses from each other. The worst of these was measles. Lies got sick on December 6 and Anne on December 10. They spoke every day on the telephone but were not allowed to meet until they were fully recovered. By Christmas, they were back to normal, but the nickname Anne had been given during her illness—"Tender One"—remained. Lies's mother, who liked Anne enormously but thought she was very full of herself, began to say of her, "God knows everything, but Anne knows everything better!"[3]

The Franks liked to entertain at home, and among their most welcome guests were Miep Santrouschitz (Mr. Frank's employee) and her friend Jan Gies, who worked for Social Services and also lived in the River Quarter. Like Miep, Jan was not Jewish, but he hated the Nazis just as much as she did. Their first evening at the Franks' apartment passed agreeably. The home was welcoming, as was the family. Soon after Miep and Jan arrived, Margot and Anne ran in from their bedroom. Margot was quite a young lady. She had the same hairstyle as her sister and wore similar clothes but looked neater than Anne, who was talkative and confident. All Anne's energy and humor seemed to be in her eyes: quick, darting eyes that were gray with electric-green flecks. Both girls had excellent manners. Miep approved of their hearty appetites and how after dinner they immediately went back to their rooms to do their homework.

By 1938, Anne's circle of friends included a number of boys. Lies was amused by her friend's flirtatious nature and her habit of twirling her hair around her

[3] Pick-Goslar, Hanneli, in Lindwer, Willy, *The Last Seven Months of Anne Frank*, Pantheon, New York, 1991, pp. 16–17.

fingers. Anne had added fashion and movie stars to her growing list of interests. At school and at parties, she was always the center of attention because she was so lively. Anne and Margot went with their father to Switzerland that year, and Buddy, Anne's cousin, remembers: "She was always ready for fun and games. We used to dress up and play film stars. Anne had a very keen sense of fairness and justice. Whenever we got dressed up and acted out our scenes, Anne never took the best garments for herself. She always gave them to me, and the funnier I looked, the better she liked it. . . . Margot was kind and sweet, but I have to admit it—I liked Anne better."[4] The 1938 vacation was great fun; Buddy and Anne dressed up in their grandmother's clothes and played with Buddy's puppet theater. But it was the last time they ever saw each other; from then on, communication was by letter alone.

In Amsterdam, Anne's father established a new company, Pectacon, which dealt in herbs and spices. He became the firm's director and appointed an old friend, Johannes Kleiman, as supervisory director and book-keeper for both Pectacon and Opekta. Mr. Frank chose a man he had often met on business trips abroad,

---

[4] Elias, Buddy, in "I Knew the Real Anne Frank," *The Mail on Sunday: You Magazine*, February 2, 1997.

Hermann van Pels, as an adviser for Pectacon. Mr. van Pels moved to Amsterdam in June 1937 with his wife and son, Peter, and eventually bought an apartment in the next street over from the Frank family. They often attended the Franks' Saturday afternoon gatherings, which were aimed at bringing German Jews together, helping them get settled, and introducing them to Dutch people.

Hermann van Pels was well-liked at the Pectacon company, where he took the orders from the sales representatives and discussed recipes with Victor Kugler, who was the staff supervisor for Pectacon as well as Opekta. Van Pels liked to joke, smoke, and drink coffee first thing in the morning before starting work.

There was one other important addition to Mr. Frank's list of employees that year: Bep Voskuijl. Bep, who was Dutch, had been born in 1919, the eldest of nine children, and she still lived at home with her parents. Tall and bespectacled, she was kindhearted and painfully shy. Bep also attended the Franks' Saturday afternoon tea parties. Among the other guests was Fritz Pfeffer, a Jewish dentist from Germany. No one had any idea then just how closely entwined all their lives would become.

In March 1939, Edith Frank's mother, Rosa

Hollander, came to live with her daughter and family in Amsterdam. Anne's uncles, Walter and Julius Hollander, emigrated to the United States, where they were able to keep in touch with the family for a time. Anne was happy to have her grandmother living with them. Grandmother Hollander, who was then seventy-three, could always spare time to listen to Anne's stories about school and friends. During the summer, she accompanied her daughter and granddaughters on day trips to the beach, and she enjoyed helping out with Anne's tenth birthday party on June 12.

Anne's last full year at the Montessori school was 1940. From the first year to the fourth, her teacher had been Mr. van Gelder. Toward the end of that time, he noticed that Anne had a new ambition: she wanted to be a writer. Anne had settled down at school by then. She worked hard, asked more questions than anyone else, and hated math but loved history, drawing, and writing essays. In her fifth year, Anne was taught by Miss Gadron, and in her final year, by the headmistress, Mrs. Kuperus. She remembered Anne well: "Anne was a very good pupil, and she took a great interest in school. . . . The last year was particularly nice. We had started to do theatricals. Anne was in her element. Of course she was full of ideas for the scripts, but since she also had no shyness and liked imitating other people, the big parts fell to her. She was rather small among her schoolmates, but when she played the queen or the princess, she suddenly seemed a good bit taller than the others."[5]

In spring 1940, Anne and Margot began writing to two pen pals in America. The exchange was arranged through a teacher. Anne's pen pal was Juanita Wagner, who lived on a farm in Danville, Iowa. In her letter, she told Anne about her home, her family, and her older sister, Betty Ann. Anne wrote back immediately:

Amsterdam, 29 April, Monday,

Dear Juanita,

I did receive your letter and want to answer you as quick as possible. Margot and myself are the only children in our house. Our grandmother is living with us. My father has an office and mother is busy at home. I live not far from school and I am in the fifth class. We have no hour classes, we may do what we prefer, of course we must get to a certain goal. Your mother will certainly know this system, it is called Montessori. We have little work at home.

---

[5] Mrs. Kuperus, "Anne was ..." in van Winsen, Matthieu, "How I Remember Anne Frank," *PRIVE*, June 16, 1979; "The last year ..." in Schnabel, Ernst, *The Footsteps of Anne Frank*, Pan Books, London, 1976, pp. 42–43.

On the map I looked again and found the name Burlington. I did ask a girl friend of mine if she would like to communicate with one of your friends. She wants to do it with a girl about my age not with a boy.

I shall write her address underneath. Did you yourself write the letter I received from you, or did your mother do it? I include a postcard from Amsterdam and shall continue to do that, collecting picture-cards. I have already about 800. A child I used to be at school with went to New York and she wrote a letter to our class some time ago. In case you and Betty get a photo do send a copy as I am curious to know how you look. My birthday is 12 June. Kindly let me know yours. Perhaps one of your friends will write first to my girl friend, for she also cannot write English but her father or mother will translate the letter.

> *Hoping to hear from you*
> *I remain*
> *Your Dutch friend*
> *Annelies Marie Frank.*

She enclosed a postcard, photos, and a letter from Margot for Betty Ann. On the postcard she had written:

> *Dear Juanita,*
> *This picture shows one of the many old canals of Amsterdam. But this is only one of the old city. There are also big canals and over all those canals are bridges. There are about 340 bridges within the city.*
> *Anne Frank.*[6]

On March 4, 1940, Anne wrote in her school friend Henny Scheerder's poetry album. Her verse, illustrated by a sticker of daisies, roses, and forget-me-nots on the same page, reads, "*It is of little worth, what I offer you, pick roses on earth and forget-me-not.*" In one corner she identified herself, "*By myself written, by myself done, Anne Frank, so is my name,*" and in the other, having read a previous entry in the book, which was dated upside down, she wrote in rhyme, "*Tip tap top, the date stands at the top.*" On the facing page, she glued in a cut-out basket of red roses and white flowers, with a dove carrying a letter in the middle. In each corner of the page, she scribbled: "*for – get – me – not.*"[7]

Otto and Edith Frank took their children to a

[6] Frank, Anne, letter and postcard, April 29, 1940. Collection of Simon Wiesenthal Center, Los Angeles, CA.
[7] Anne Frank verse in article by Isaak Gluck, Peggy, *The Jewish Journal: Anne Frank's Signature*, April 20–26, 1990, and in *Holy Land Treasures: Antique Judaica, Rare Anne Frank Autograph Verse*, 1990.

professional photographer every year to record their growing up. The photos taken of Anne in 1940 show her sitting hunched up, her arms folded, with her hair pinned up at the sides. She smiles in most of the pictures and captioned them: "Things are getting more serious but there's still a smile left over for the funny bits," "Oh, what a joke!" "Whatever next?" "That's a funny story."[8] In one photograph, she lifts her head slightly and seems to be deep in thought. She wrote beside it: "This is a photograph of me as I wish I looked all the time. Then I might still have a chance of getting to Holywood [Anne's spelling of Hollywood]. But at present, I'm afraid, I usually look quite different." [9]

On May 10, 1940, Germany invaded the Netherlands. Four days later the Dutch forces surrendered. As of that date, the Netherlands was completely under German rule.

---

[8] *Anne Frank's Diary*, undated.
[9] *Anne Frank's Diary*, October 10, 1942.

Chapter Three:
Everything Is Forbidden

"Now that the Germans rule the roost here, we are in real trouble. ..."
(*Anne Frank's Diary*, June 15, 1942)

At first, life in Amsterdam after the invasion continued much as it always had. Anne and her friends Sanne and Lies now liked to sit in the square reading fashion magazines, discussing movie stars, and giggling about boys. A young neighbor, Eva Geiringer, remembers: "Anne flirted with boys and had boyfriends. She looked very modern and was always smiling. Margot, Anne's sister, didn't push herself forward. Edith was the same, friendly, but not the sort to make an impression. Otto was like Anne, very outgoing. You could feel a warmth coming from him."[1]

During the summer, the Franks went on many weekend walks around Amsterdam, enjoying the

[1] Schloss, Eva, author interview, London, January 1998.

beautiful weather. They still saw the Goslars very often. Lies's father played a trick on Anne's parents: he made himself up like Hitler, brushing his black hair forward over his forehead and styling his mustache, then rang their doorbell. The Franks were horrified at first, thinking that Hitler was paying them a private visit, but they started to laugh when they realized it was Hans Goslar.

On December 1, 1940, Anne's father's businesses, Opekta and Pectacon, moved to 263 Prinsengracht, in the Jordaan district of Amsterdam. Today it is famous for being the place where Anne Frank and her family went into hiding, but at that time it was just a business address. The ground floor of the building was used as a warehouse, while the first floor became the offices. A steep staircase led up to the second floor, where large mixing containers, sacks of jam-making ingredients, and spices were kept. The attics above were also used for storage. As in many canal-side houses, there was an annexe at the back. The second and third floors of the annexe were not used, but Anne's father converted the open space on the first floor into two rooms for his private office and the staff kitchen.

The Nazis were then closing down businesses run by Jews, so Otto Frank did two things to keep his companies safe. He changed the name of Pectacon, with Jan Gies's help, to Gies & Co. and pretended that he was no longer the head of the company. He did a similar thing with Opekta, resigning from the company and allowing Johannes Kleiman to take his position. In fact, Anne's father was as much in charge as he had ever been, but the Nazis, who did not know this, ignored Pectacon and Opekta, leaving them to carry on as usual.

At the beginning of 1941, Anne wrote two letters to Switzerland, mainly about her passion for skating. She told her cousins: "Every spare minute I am at the ice rink. . . . I'm taking regular lessons and I do waltzing, jumping, in fact everything to do with ice skating. . . . If I can skate really well, Daddy has promised me a trip to Switzerland to see you all."[2] But soon a law was passed by the German authorities forbidding Jews to ice-skate. Anne never received her reward, and it would have been impossible anyway because all travel across the borders of occupied territory was also forbidden.

June 12, 1941, was Anne's twelfth birthday. Although there were many places she could no longer visit as a Jewish girl, her parents made sure she was able to enjoy the activities that were still open to her. There were more day trips with her friends, and in the summer

---

[2] Frank, Anne, letter, January 13, 1941. Private collection of Buddy Elias.

she went to a children's holiday camp with Sanne. Her parents and sister joined her for a while before returning to Amsterdam and the news that Miep and Jan were getting married. They were all invited, but Anne's grandmother was seriously ill, and Margot was also sick, so Anne's mother stayed at home to care for them. Anne and her father, though, were thrilled to be among the guests at the wedding on July 16, 1941, in the city's town hall. Anne wore a new dress and jacket, and a matching hat with a ribbon. Her hair had been cut and styled into a chin-length bob for the occasion, and she looked every inch the smart young girl her friends so admired.

The newlyweds visited the Franks at home shortly afterward, and Miep noticed how the two girls were affected by the changes taking place in Amsterdam. Margot was often sick and was quieter than ever, but still kind and sweet. Anne was even more talkative in contrast, and chattered on about school, movie stars, her friends, and boyfriends. On August 29, a new law came into effect that altered their lives completely: Jewish children were no longer allowed to attend the same schools as non-Jews. All the Jewish children at Anne's school were called in to a special assembly and told that they would not be returning in the new school year. Anne and Margot were very upset by the move: it made it especially hard for them to keep their friendships with the non-Jewish children they knew. They were both transferred to the Jewish Lyceum, a three-story building with a long concrete playground at the front and one at the back. An archway under the neighboring houses led through to the Amstel River. Anne went into the First Form of the Lyceum with Lies Goslar, and Margot went into the Fourth with her best friend, Jetteke Frijda.

Anne found a new best friend at the Lyceum, Jacqueline van Maarsen, who lived with her parents and sister in the River Quarter. Jacque's father was Jewish by birth, which meant that the family was affected by the anti-Semitic laws. Jacque met Anne after their first day at the Lyceum. She was cycling home when someone called out after her, and she turned to see Anne waving at her. Anne pedaled up on her bike and introduced herself brightly. "We can bicycle home together from now on. I live at Merwedeplein."[3] On the way back she talked nonstop, telling Jacque all about her friends at her old school, then invited her in to meet her family. The two girls had shared interests: they liked to read the

---

[3] van Maarsen, Jacqueline, *My Friend Anne Frank,* Vantage Press, New York, 1996, p. 6.

same books, were fascinated by mythology, and loved to play board games and to look at their collection of movie-star postcards. Anne's house became a mini local theater where she and Jacque organized shows, with her father in charge of the projector and her mother handing out refreshments. They even sent out tickets to everyone! Despite living so close together, Anne and Jacque would often spend the night at each other's house. Whenever Anne went to stay with Jacque, she took along a suitcase and a cosmetic case with her curlers and hairbrush. The suitcase was empty, but Anne always took it, because then she felt as though she really was going away!

Shortly after Jacque and Anne first met, Anne and her father went on a short trip to Arnhem. Otto Frank explained in a postcard: "We're not staying long, I just wanted to have a bit more peace and quiet but didn't want to go off completely on my own. Anne is always good, dear company and she was able to have a few days off school. Everything is well." The front of the card showed their hotel, and across it Anne wrote happily, "We're staying here! In the middle of the forest! Isn't it wonderful?"[4]

---

[4] Frank, Otto, and Frank, Anne, postcard, September 14, 1941. Private collection of Buddy Elias.

In January 1942, Anne's grandmother died of cancer. The whole family was very upset, and Anne missed her company a great deal. On January 20, the Franks applied to the authorities for emigration to England. Hermann van Pels also made an application to move his family to America, but in reply to their requests, both families received letters informing them that their applications were postponed until further notice. In April 1942, the Franks and the van Pelses celebrated the Jewish festival of Passover together, but their thoughts were on the future. Otto Frank and Hermann van Pels decided that the best way to avoid being sent away to the concentration camps in eastern Europe would be to go into hiding. The annexe at 263 Prinsengracht would serve as a hiding place, provided Kugler, Kleiman, Bep, and Miep would be willing to keep their secret and take care of them. All four agreed immediately, even though they knew that the punishment for helping Jews was imprisonment or death.

Preparations began. The annexe was thoroughly cleaned out and cleared of trash. Food, bedclothes, soap, towels, and kitchen utensils were easy to move. Furniture and other large items were picked up in a van and taken to the hiding place after office hours. All work done in the annexe took place gradually, on weekends or in the evening. Paper was pasted over the windows in the front house facing the annexe, shielding the rooms from the warehousemen and visitors to the office. The families would move in sometime during July 1942.

Anne and Margot were not told immediately about the hiding plan: their father wanted them to enjoy what was left of their freedom. Although there were a lot of restrictions on their lives, Jewish children worked around these difficulties as best they could. For instance, they were not allowed in any sports halls, so they played Ping-Pong at home instead. Anne, Lies, Jacque, Sanne, and another friend named Ilse formed their own club, playing games in the dining room of Ilse's home with her Ping-Pong set. Afterward, they usually walked to an ice-cream shop, where they could sit outside and flirt with boys. Anne's father could see that his younger daughter was enjoying herself with her friends, and he later wrote: "She was always on the go, and always brought a whole community of children with her wherever she was. People loved her because she always had ideas, what to play, where to play, some new thing to do. . . . Anne had one quality that was a bit annoying. She was constantly asking questions, not only when we were alone, but also in the presence of others. When we had visitors, it was very difficult to get rid of her, because everyone and everything was of interest to her."[5]

When Anne wrote to congratulate Buddy on his seventeenth birthday, she told him: "We've had five days' holiday for Whitsun, it was great and I've been busy every day. This evening I won't get home until 10 P.M., but I'm usually escorted home by a young man. How's it going with your girlfriend, the one you sent a picture of? Please write more about her, things like that always interest me. Margot also has a boyfriend, but he's even younger than mine!"[6]

Friday, June 12, was Anne's own birthday, her thirteenth. Her favorite gift was from her father: a small red-and-white checked book to use as a diary. Lies arrived early that morning to collect Anne for school and admired the diary briefly before Anne put it away in her bedroom. In the living room, all Anne's other presents were on display and there were flowers everywhere. In the kitchen, her mother was baking a strawberry tart, while her father sat comfortably in his chair and shared a joke with Lies as usual. When it was time to leave, Mrs. Frank gave Anne a basket of sweet

---

[5] Frank, Otto, memoir. Private collection of Buddy Elias.
[6] Frank, Anne, letter, May 1942. Private collection of Buddy Elias.

biscuits to hand out at school, and Anne added some biscuits she had made. In the afternoon, Lies, Jacque, Sanne, and Ilse gave Anne their joint gift, a book called *Tales and Legends of the Netherlands.*

At some point on June 12, Anne wrote in her diary for the first time. She pasted in a school photograph of herself from winter 1941 with the caption, "Gorgeous photograph, isn't it!!!!"[7] At the front of the book she wrote: "I hope that I shall be able to confide in you completely, as I have never been able to do in anyone before, and I hope that you will be a great support and comfort to me."[8] All Anne's friends knew that she had been given a diary, but she never allowed anyone to see what she had written.

Anne's birthday party was held at home on the Sunday after her birthday. Lies remembers the scores of children there; Anne's parents handing out strawberry tart on china plates; glasses of cool milk for everyone; Margot and her friend Jetteke joining in with them all; the shades being pulled down as Mr. Frank set up the projector and then *Rin-Tin-Tin and the Lighthouse Keeper* whirring into life on the blank wall. She also remembers having to leave the party early to help her mother with

[7] *Anne Frank's Diary*, June 12, 1942.

[8] *Anne Frank's Diary*, June 12, 1942.

Gabi (her baby sister) and how jealous she felt when she saw Anne and Jacque whispering together. There were several quarrels among their group of friends, but the arguments never lasted long.

By the end of June, Anne had a new boyfriend, Hello Silverberg. Hello was also from Germany and had arrived in the River Quarter in 1938. He lived with his grandparents and was a handsome sixteen-year-old when his cousin introduced him to Anne. He remembers, "She was very attractive and she liked to laugh and to make people laugh. She was very entertaining and extremely lively. She did little imitations of people that were very clever. In my memory I always see her sitting in a big chair, with her hands under her chin and looking directly at whomever she was with. . . . I think I was probably in love with her. She seemed to think so too."[9] Anne's parents liked Hello, but his grandparents disapproved of her. She worried about this and questioned him about their future together. He told her: "Love finds a way!"

At the end of the school year, the children received their examination results. Margot's were excellent as

[9] Silverberg, Edmond, "She was very ..." author telephone interview, June 1998; "I think I was probably ..." in Traster, Tina, "Holocaust Survivor Discloses His Courtship of Anne Frank," *The Record* (Hackensack, N.J.), April 18, 1996.

usual, and Anne's were better than she had expected, although she and Lies would have to retake the math exam in September. Around this time, Anne heard about the hiding plan from her father (Margot already knew). Anne wrote in her diary that she hoped the day when they had to disappear was a long way off. In fact, it was much closer than any of them could have guessed.

The morning of Sunday, July 5, 1942, was sunny and hot. Anne's father walked to a Jewish hospital where he knew some of the elderly patients, leaving Margot and Anne at home with their mother. Hello stopped by to ask Anne to go out with him later that day. When he had gone, Anne stretched out on the balcony to read. At 3 P.M. the doorbell rang and there was a call from the street, "Miss Margot Frank?" Mrs. Frank went down, and a policeman handed her a brown envelope. Inside was a card ordering Margot to report to the SS the next morning.

The card was one of thousands sent out that day to German Jews in Amsterdam. Four thousand Jews were to be deported to German "work camps" between July 14 and July 17, 1942. Most were boys and girls aged fifteen and sixteen. Along with the card was a list of clothing to be packed in a knapsack. Mrs. Frank left home immediately to tell the van Pelses the hiding plan had to be brought forward. At first, Margot told Anne that the

SS had sent a call-up for their father, but then she told her the truth. Anne began to cry. Neither girl spoke because the heat and the terror were overwhelming. Hello returned at the same time as their mother and Hermann van Pels. He was told that Anne could not see him just then, and Jacque was told something similar when she telephoned later. Anne and Margot were sent to their room to begin packing. Anne put her diary and old letters into a satchel. They were more important to her than clothes. She still did not know where their hiding place would be.

Anne's father returned at 5 P.M. and, when he was given the news, called Kleiman, who came over to see what he could do. Miep and Jan arrived to take the Franks' belongings to their own home for safekeeping until they were in the hiding place. An atmosphere of panic and fear made everyone much quieter than usual. The Franks' lodger, Goldschmidt, called on them (he knew nothing of the hiding plan). He stayed until 10 P.M. At 11 P.M., Miep and Jan returned to take away more items and clothing. When they had gone, Anne's father wrote to his family in Switzerland, hinting that they were going into hiding: "It's a pity that we can no longer correspond with you, but that's how it is. You must understand." Anne added her last greetings: "I cannot write a letter about the holidays now. Regards and kisses from Anne."[10] It was 11:30 P.M. when they went to bed. Anne was exhausted and fell asleep immediately.

It was raining the next morning as the family ate breakfast in the semi-darkness at 5:30 A.M. They each wore as much clothing as possible to lessen the amount they had to carry. Margot filled her satchel with schoolbooks and pulled out her bike to wait for Miep, who arrived at 6:00 A.M. on her bicycle. They rode off across Merwedeplein silently. Mr. and Mrs. Frank left a letter for Goldschmidt, asking him to take Anne's cat, Moortje, to their neighbors. Then they stripped the beds and scattered the breakfast things on the table as if they had had to leave suddenly. At 7:30 A.M., they set off on foot in the warm rain. The streets were still dark and cars sped by, their headlights blurred by the downpour. As they walked, Anne's father told her about the hiding place.

Miep and Margot were the first to arrive at the annexe. Margot was close to fainting. Miep took her quickly up to the annexe before going downstairs to the front office. When Anne and her parents reached the building later that morning, drenched by the rain and tired from the

---

[10] Frank, Anne, postcard, July 5, 1942. Private collection of Buddy Elias.

long walk, they went straight upstairs to the annexe. It was a mess, with boxes and sacks piled everywhere. In Mr. and Mrs. Frank's bedroom/living room there were two divans, three tables, bookshelves, a built-in closet, and 150 cans of food. A window overlooked the courtyard below and the houses opposite. A door to the right led to Anne and Margot's narrow room. It had a window, two divan beds, and three built-in closets. Next door was a washroom with a toilet. A doorway on the right led back into the passageway and to the entrance door. On the floor above was a large room with double windows looking out onto the courtyard again. This was set aside for Mr. and Mrs. van Pels. It was almost bare, apart from a sink, closets, a gas stove, two beds, and a table. Another door led into the tiny damp room where Peter van Pels would sleep. There was a small shuttered window facing the front house, and the stairs to the attic in the middle of the room, along with a bed and a closet. From the arched side-window in the attic, the tower of the Westerkirk (West Church) could be seen.

Visiting the annexe later that day, Miep found Mrs. Frank and Margot lying on their beds, but Anne and her father were busy trying to get things organized as quietly as possible. Miep could not imagine how they must have felt, but she was upset to see her friends forced to leave their home, their possessions, and their other friends. By then, the Franks' neighbors on Merwedeplein knew that they had gone. Everyone was saddened to lose the Franks but not surprised, because other families who had received the call-up notice had also disappeared. Mr. Frank had left out a letter for their lodger to see, which falsely hinted that they were in Switzerland. Goldschmidt told Anne's friends this when they came to call for her and he handed them Moortje, her cat. Jacque and Lies were very upset when they found out. Goldschmidt let them into the apartment when they explained that they wanted to find something of Anne's to keep. Jacque remembers going into Anne's bedroom and seeing "Anne's unmade bed and on the floor in front of it, her new shoes, as if they had just been kicked off. . . . I saw Variety, the game she had just got for her birthday and which we had played like crazy the past few weeks, just lying there. . . ."[11] They found Anne's swimming medals and took them—a few small reminders of the friend who had vanished.

---

[11] van Maarsen, Jacqueline, *My Friend Anne Frank*, Vantage Press, New York, 1996, pp. 27–28.

Chapter Four:
In Hiding

"Hiding has become quite an everyday word. ..."
(*Anne Frank's Diary*, May 2, 1943)

Anne Frank and her family were among 25,000 Jews who went into hiding during the German occupation of the Netherlands. People hid wherever they could, in towns or in the country.

Jews in hiding were completely dependent upon the people who hid them. Many of these helpers were members of the Resistance (people working secretly against the Nazis), and the families they hid had to keep moving to new hiding places to ensure that they were not betrayed or discovered. Anne and her family were lucky: the people who hid them were old friends, and they tried their best to make things as easy as possible for the people in their care. Anne often wrote about the helpers in her diary: "Never have we heard one word of the burden which we certainly must be to them, never has one of them complained about all the trouble we cause. They all come upstairs every day, talk to the men about business and politics, to the women about food and wartime difficulties, and about newspapers and books with the children. They put on the brightest possible faces, bring flowers and presents for birthdays and bank holidays, are always ready to help and do all they can."[1]

In all, eight people hid in the secret annexe: Anne and her family, the van Pelses, and, from November 1942, the dentist Fritz Pfeffer. They had to be extremely careful that no one else, apart from their helpers, knew they were there. The door to the secret annexe was concealed by a special bookcase that could be moved by those who knew where to look for its hidden hinges. Windows were covered by strips of thick material and blackout boards, used by everyone during wartime to confuse the enemy bombers. There were certain rules that had to be strictly observed: the eight in hiding had to be as quiet as possible during office hours; the curtains were kept closed; the toilet was out of bounds when anyone else was in the building; and so on. Their fears of discovery were made worse by a number of burglaries that

---

[1] *Anne Frank's Diary*, January 28, 1944.

occurred at the offices during the period in hiding, and by the arrival in the warehouse of a new staff member, who was obviously very curious about the hiding place. Anne wrote about this man, Willem Gerard van Maaren, several times in her diary, wondering if he would ever betray them.

Apart from the fear of being discovered, the biggest worry in hiding was food. Every morning, Miep and Bep gave the families their rations, which they collected on their behalf. Bread was purchased from a friend of Kleiman, and a friend of van Pels provided them with meat. Miep visited a grocery store nearby for vegetables and became friendly with the owner, who was in the Dutch Resistance. He soon guessed the reason for Miep's frequent visits to his shop but never gave away her secret. Bep was responsible for the milk ration and smuggled several bottles a day from the office supply to the annexe. She also provided fruit for her friends in hiding when the prices were low. The attic quickly became a food store: potatoes, peas, and other vegetables were kept there, along with lots of canned foods. In her diary, Anne sometimes grumbles about the lengthy food "cycles" they had to endure—weeks when only one or two types of food were available to them. As the war dragged on, Miep often spent hours in line for groceries, only to be told at the counter that there was nothing left. Several big arguments broke out in the annexe over the poor food and the way in which it was divided among them all.

There were other practical difficulties besides food. Soap, for example, was hard to find in the shops, so Miep and Bep had to give them what they could spare from their own rations once the original supply had dwindled. Washing was not a problem, since there was a sink in the annexe, but taking a bath proved a little more difficult. Privacy was the main concern: each person chose his or her own place, using a portable tin washtub. Anne and Margot occasionally used the front office after hours but had to wash themselves in semi-darkness so that no one passing by in the street would see them. Electricity had to be used sparingly because when their rations ran out they were left without light or warmth. In that situation they had to use candles to enable them to see and pile coats on the beds at night to ward off the cold. When it was dark and they had no electricity, they amused themselves and kept warm by exercising and dancing. Illness was another cause for alarm because, of course, they could not call a doctor. In winter 1943, Anne had a high fever brought on by influenza, and all kinds of potions and remedies were used to cure her.

May 1925: Anne's parents, Otto and Edith, on their honeymoon in San Remo, Italy.

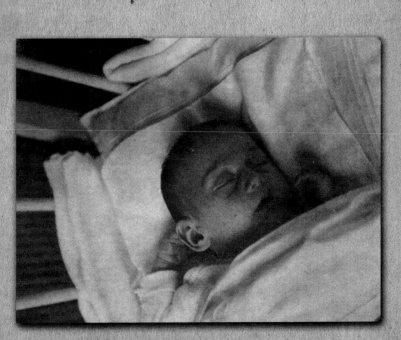

Summer 1929: Anne Frank soon after her birth.

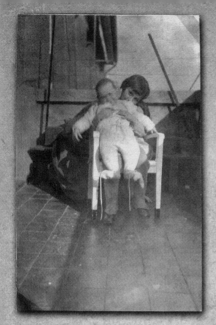

1929 – 1930: Margot Frank cuddles her new sister, Anne, on the balcony of their home in Frankfurt.

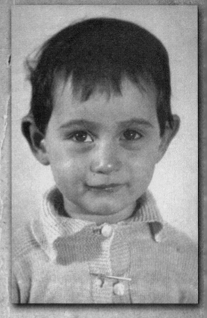

1932: Anne, the smiling toddler.

1931 – 1932 Anne being fed by her mother while her sister, Margot, and cousin Stephan look on.

1934: Margot, Anne, and their mother enjoy a day out at the beach in Zandvoort. The woman in the background is Mrs. Schneider, Otto Frank's secretary from Frankfurt.

1934 – 1935
Anne and one of her best friends, Sanne Ledermann, on the Merwedeplein, where they lived.

1940: Anne and Margot at the beach in Zandvoort again. Anne is eleven years old in the photo.

1935: Anne on vacation in Sils–Maria.

1935: Anne at school; she is in the middle of the classroom at the back.

263 Prinsengracht. The Secret Annexe. Anne's room is the middle window on the left.

1935 – 1942:
Anne Frank growing up.

Anne toont haar
nieuwe jas.

July 1941: Anne in the outfit she wore to Miep's wedding. She captioned this photo herself, "Anne tries on her new coat."

MR. KOOPHUIS

Mr. Kleiman standing in front of the swinging bookcase. The photograph was taken after the war.

Peter van Pels

MARGOT
FRANK
1926–1945
ANNE
FRANK
1929–1945

1999: Buddy Elias, first cousin of Anne and Margot, watches over the erecting of a memorial stone for them at Bergen-Belsen.

Being cramped in a few small rooms with no chance to escape affected them all. Squabbles broke out over minor matters, and relationships grew extremely strained. Most of the arguments were about food, but other things also caused trouble. Mr. and Mrs. van Pels had some furious disagreements about money, while Mrs. Frank and Mrs. van Pels argued endlessly about bringing up children. Mrs. van Pels and Anne also had numerous quarrels, usually over Anne's "cheekiness."

Despite the frequent arguments, there were also many humorous moments in hiding. Hermann van Pels loved to tell jokes, and both Anne and Peter enjoyed dressing up for a giggle in their parents' clothes—Anne in her father's suit, Peter in one of his mother's dresses. Any cause for celebration was welcomed in the annexe. Birthdays, religious festivals, good news of the war—all were greeted with enormous pleasure. The helpers often joined in the celebrations and even threw a surprise party in the annexe at the end of 1942 to welcome the New Year. Such occasions made life a little less dull.

Everyone in hiding tried to keep himself or herself as quietly busy as possible through the day: studying, sewing, writing, reading. To her annoyance, Anne was not always allowed to read the same books as Margot and Peter, but she loved biographies, mythology, and romance. She compiled royal family trees and studied shorthand with Margot and Peter. Mr. Frank made sure that the three teenagers did not miss out on their education by tutoring them in a variety of subjects, including languages, algebra, geometry, geography, and history. The attic became a peaceful spot for individual study. Anne also used it as a writing room, and Peter made himself a carpentry workshop in one corner. After her lessons and at night, Anne sometimes relieved her boredom by borrowing her father's binoculars and zooming in on the houses opposite the courtyard. Past the black skeleton of the chestnut tree, she could see a dentist's surgery, where the patient one evening was an elderly woman who was "awfully scared."[2]

Young as she was and courageous, Anne viewed being in hiding as a great adventure. She compared it in her diary to being on vacation in a very strange hotel and made the best of a terrible situation, but at night, fear got the better of her, and in the silence her imagination ran wild. The minutes crawled by, and each creak and movement made her wonder if they had been discovered. Planes flew past, firing at the enemy in the dark, and she was sure that the annexe would be hit by a

---

[2] *Anne Frank's Diary*, November 28, 1942.

bomb. Nighttime terrors aside, she often wrote about how lucky she felt to be in hiding with people she knew, cared for by friends. She only really became downhearted when she thought about her old life, her friends, and her cat, Moortje, whom she missed very much. She wrote then how miserable she was: "When someone comes in from outside, with the wind in their clothes and the cold air on their faces, then I could bury my head in the blankets to stop myself thinking: When will we be granted the privilege of smelling fresh air . . . ? Cycling, dancing, whistling, looking out into the world, feeling young, to know that I am free—that's what I long for. . . ."[3] She escaped into daydreams of "after the war" but found that the best way of overcoming her fears and sadness was to go up into the attic, where the window was open. There she could gaze at the sky and the tower of the Westerkirk. Staring at the chestnut tree "on whose branches little raindrops shone, at the seagulls and other birds that looked like silver in the sun,"[4] brought her peace for a while.

The helpers tried to protect their friends from the reality of life on the outside, the deportations and the cruelties, but it was impossible to keep everything secret.

[3] *Anne Frank's Diary*, December 24, 1943.
[4] *Anne Frank's Diary*, February 23, 1944.

Besides, the people in hiding wanted to know the truth, however bad it was. They listened to the radio regularly and heard reports on the Dutch station, Radio Oranje, of Jews being killed by shooting and poisoned to death by gas. They tried hard to keep their spirits up, despite the horror of it all, by keeping to their routine and burying themselves in work and hobbies. Anne wrote in her diary very sensibly, "It won't do us any good or help those outside to go on being as gloomy as we are at the moment. . . . Must I keep thinking about those other people whatever I am doing and if I want to laugh about something, should I stop myself quickly and feel ashamed that I am cheerful? Ought I then to cry the whole day long? No, that I can't do. . . ."[5]

The persecutions made them more aware than ever before of their Jewish identity. Of the eight in hiding, Pfeffer was the most religious, but they all observed the major festivals, enjoyed traditional Jewish food when it was available, and welcomed in the Sabbath every Friday night. Anne's interest in her religion increased as she got older. She had nightmares about the fate of the Jews in Europe, and in her dreams she saw her friend Lies dressed in rags, starving and crying for help. For Anne,

---

[5] *Anne Frank's Diary*, November 20, 1942.

Lies became a symbol of Jewish persecution, and in her diary she wrote how wicked she felt to be sleeping in a warm bed while her friends were suffering: "I get frightened when I think of close friends who have now been delivered into the hands of the cruelest brutes the world has ever seen. And all because they are Jews."[6]

Anne was frequently upset about other things too, including her relationship with her mother. The two had many arguments, which were largely the result of the pressures of being in hiding and Anne's need for independence (she felt that her mother treated her like a baby). Anne's father tried his best to keep the peace between his wife and daughter, but in the end it was Anne herself who learned to have more patience with her mother and to try to see things from her viewpoint for a change.

Being in hiding did not prevent Anne from taking care and pride in her appearance. She pin-curled her hair in the same style as Margot and made a combing-shawl out of rose-patterned material, which she tied under her chin to catch stray hairs when she brushed out her curls. She dreamed of being able to buy lots of makeup and clothes after the war, writing out a list of what she thought she would need in her diary. She

---

[6] *Anne Frank's Diary*, November 19, 1942.

studied the angles of her face in the mirror and wondered whether she was attractive (Margot told her she had "nice eyes"). From time to time, everyone tried to make a real fuss of her, knowing it was very difficult for such a lively young girl to put up with the quiet and loneliness of life in hiding. She noticed that Peter was becoming more interested in her, and when he looked at her she was happy and excited. Soon he was confiding in her, which was exactly what she wanted. They spent hours in the attic together, sitting by the window and looking out at the Westerkirk or across the courtyard and watching winter turn to spring on the chestnut tree. Gradually the intense feelings Anne had for Peter began to fade, however; he could not satisfy her need to talk about "deeper" subjects, and he was not as intelligent as she was.

In 1944, Anne wrote at length in her diary about how she had changed since her birthday in 1942. She now felt that she was a young woman, one who wanted something different from the lives led by other women she knew, something more than a husband and family (though she wanted those too): "Although I'm only fourteen, I know quite well what I want, I know who is right and who is wrong, I have my opinions, my own ideas and principles, and although it may sound pretty mad from an adolescent, I feel more of a person than a child, I feel quite independent of anyone. . . ."[7] Anne realized that part of the reason she had grown up so quickly was because of the life she was being forced to lead: "My start has been so very full of interest, and that is the sole reason why I have to laugh at the comical side of the most dangerous moments. I am young and I possess many buried qualities; I am young and strong and am living a great adventure. . . ."[8] She sometimes found it hard to be so optimistic, but with a struggle, she succeeded: "It's really a wonder I haven't dropped all my ideals, because they seem so absurd and impossible to carry out. Yet I keep them because, in spite of everything, I still believe that people are really good at heart."[9]

Anne's diary was a great comfort to her, just as she had hoped it would be. She usually wrote in it in her parents' room, in her own room, or at the desk by the window in the attic. Everyone in hiding knew Anne was keeping a diary because she often asked them not to disturb her while she was writing, and she sometimes read aloud from it, though no one ever tried

---

[7] *Anne Frank's Diary*, March 17, 1944.

[8] *Anne Frank's Diary*, May 3, 1944.

[9] *Anne Frank's Diary*, July 15, 1944.

to read it without her permission. When the original diary her father had bought her was full, the helpers gave her office books and loose sheets of paper to write on. In summer 1943, Anne began to write short stories.[10] Some of these, such as "The Battle of the Potatoes" and "Villains," are essays about the daily routine in the annexe. "Villains!" concerned the problem of fleas in the hiding place, although the villains were not the fleas, but the van Pelses, who had ignored the advice they had been given about how to get rid of the tiny pests, resulting in an outbreak of itchiness. Other stories, such as "Kitty," "The Porter's Family," and "Eva's Dream," are more like fairy tales. Anne kept a record of all her non-diary work in an oblong office cashbook, providing an index and details of when the stories were written. Sometimes she read aloud from this book to her companions and the helpers.

At the start of 1944, Anne was already thinking about what would happen to her diary after the war. "I trust to luck, but should I be saved, and spared from destruction, then it would be terrible if my diaries and my tales were lost."[11] Her writing, she felt, was the finest

---

[10] Frank, Anne, *Tales from the Secret Annexe*, Penguin, London, 1982.
[11] *Anne Frank's Diary*, February 3, 1944.

thing she had, and she now knew what she wanted to do when the war was over and she had completed her education: "I want to write later on, and even if I don't become a writer I won't neglect my writing while doing some other job. Oh yes, I don't want to have lived for nothing like most people. I want to go on living after my death! And therefore I am grateful to God for giving me this gift, this possibility of developing myself and of writing, of expressing all that is in me."[12]

On March 28, 1944, Anne was listening to Radio Oranje. A speech by the Dutch Minister for Education, Art, and Science urged people to keep all their personal documents, such as diaries and letters, safe. When the war was over, these would then be stored in a special center so that future generations could learn how ordinary people had been forced to live. The other occupants of the annexe immediately turned to Anne and began talking excitedly about her diary. Anne herself was thrilled by the idea and began rewriting her whole diary with a view to publication. On May 11, she started work properly on the task of adapting her diary into a book she wanted to call *Het Achterhuis* ("The House Behind"). The new version was written on sheets

---

[12] *Anne Frank's Diary*, April 4, 1944.

of colored carbon paper. Anne altered parts of what she had originally written, deleted some details, added others, and combined a number of entries. She drew up a list of name changes for everyone she had mentioned, calling herself "Anne Robin." On June 12, 1944, Anne turned fifteen, and as a present, Miep and Bep gave her a collection of unused office ledgers in which to write. Anne asked Bep then about the possibility of sending her stories off to magazines under another name. When Bep asked her if she really wanted to be a writer, she said, "Yes . . . no . . . yes . . ." then answered with a sudden, brilliant smile, "No, I want to marry early and have lots of children!"[13]

Two months later, on August 1, Anne wrote her last letter to Kitty. She ended it: ". . . if I'm quiet and serious, everyone thinks it's a new comedy and then I have to get out of it by turning it into a joke, not to mention my own family, who are sure to think I'm ill, make me swallow pills for headaches and nerves, feel my neck and my head to see whether I'm running a temperature, ask me if I'm constipated and criticize me for being in a bad mood. I can't keep that up: if I'm watched to that extent, I start by getting snappy, then unhappy, and finally I

[13] Voskuijl, Bep, in Schnabel, Ernst, *The Footsteps of Anne Frank*, Pan Books, London, 1976, p. 90.

twist my heart around again, so that the bad is on the outside and the good is on the inside, and keep on trying to find a way of becoming what I would so like to be and what I could be, if . . . there weren't any other people living in the world. Yours, Anne M. Frank."[14]

Three days later, on August 4, 1944, the eight people in the secret annexe were betrayed.

---

[14] *Anne Frank's Diary*, August 1, 1944.

Chapter Five:
Capture

"I am afraid of prison cells and concentration camps. . . ."
(*Anne Frank's Diary*, March 12, 1944)

It was a warm, still summer's day. By midmorning on August 4, 1944, everyone in the secret annexe was in his or her usual place. They were reading or studying quietly; in the offices below, Miep, Bep, Kleiman, and Kugler were working at routine tasks, and on the ground floor the warehousemen were mixing and packing spices. At about 10:30 A.M., a car pulled up in front of the building. Several men got out, and one of them asked the warehouseman standing at the door a question. He pointed upstairs, and the men went inside.

In the front office, Miep, Bep, and Kleiman all looked up as the door opened, having heard footsteps on the stairs. A man stood before them, not in uniform, but holding a gun nevertheless. He told them not to move and then went through to the next office, where Kugler was working.

Kugler glanced up. Several Dutch Nazis stood in the doorway, all in ordinary clothes apart from their leader, Karl Josef Silberbauer, who wore the uniform of the Gestapo—the Nazi secret police. He asked Kugler who was in charge of the offices.

"I am," Kugler replied.

One of the other men stepped forward. "We know *everything*," he said. "You're hiding Jews and they're in this building. Take us to them."

Kugler felt the blood rush to his face. He knew it was over. He got up and led the way upstairs. When they reached the corridor where the bookcase hid the entrance to the secret annexe, he pretended that there was nothing else to see. The Nazis shook the bookcase until they found the hook holding it against the wall. They lifted it from its latch, and the door to the annexe was revealed. Silberbauer drew his gun and pushed Kugler in before him.

In the Franks' sitting room, Anne's mother stood alone, beside the table. She looked anxious and confused by Kugler's unexpected appearance. "The Gestapo are here," Kugler said.

The Gestapo now entered the other secret rooms, rounding everyone up. Mr. Frank and Peter were the last to know that they had been discovered. They were studying English in Peter's room when a man walked in and pointed a pistol at them. Neither of them said anything; the shock was too great. They followed the man into the van Pelses' room, where Mr. and Mrs. van Pels and Fritz Pfeffer stood with their hands above their heads. Another Nazi ordered them downstairs to the first floor of the annexe.

Anne stood silently with her mother and sister in the middle of their sitting room, hands raised. Margot wept softly. The sun glittered through the thick blackout curtains. Silberbauer turned to Anne's father and asked him where they kept their valuables. Mr. Frank pointed to a closet. Silberbauer lifted out a small cashbox containing a few pieces of jewelry and some money. He glanced about, and his gaze fell on Mr. Frank's briefcase. He picked it up and shook it open. Notebooks, loose papers, and a check-covered autograph album fell to the floor: Anne's diary. Anne said nothing. Silberbauer emptied the cashbox into the briefcase, then added a few other items. "Have you any weapons?" he asked, snapping the briefcase shut.

They all shook their heads. "Good," Silberbauer said.

"Now get ready. I want everyone back here in five minutes."

It did not take long for them to pack their small "emergency" bags, which they had always intended to use if a bomb hit the annexe and they needed to escape in a hurry. While everyone was doing that, Silberbauer asked Anne's father how long they had been in hiding. When Mr. Frank told him it was just over two years, Silberbauer could hardly believe him. Anne's father showed him some pencil lines drawn on one wall, along with letters and dates, and said, "That's where we've measured the height of my younger daughter while we've been here." Silberbauer was further surprised when Mr. Frank told him he had been a lieutenant in the German Army during World War I. His manner seemed to change slightly from that moment. He told everyone they could take their time packing their things, and told his men to allow them some space to do this.

When they had all gathered their belongings, Silberbauer ordered them along the corridor to the swinging bookcase. When they were all in the hallway, one of the Nazis locked the door and shoved the bookcase into place. They went downstairs into the private office and stood there silently. Silberbauer fired questions, first at Kugler, then at Kleiman. Their answer was always: "I have nothing to say." Silberbauer's temper eventually snapped, and he told them he was arresting them too. The prisoners were then ordered to go outside.

A group of curious onlookers had gathered around the waiting police van in front of the warehouse. Among them were the warehouse clerks, who said nothing to each other or to the people climbing into the van. The doors slammed shut and darkness fell around them.

Following their arrest, the Franks, the van Pelses, Pfeffer, Kugler, and Kleiman were taken to the Gestapo headquarters in southern Amsterdam. They were locked in a room with a number of other prisoners. After a while, Kugler and Kleiman were taken to another cell. With the exception of Otto Frank, they never saw their friends alive again.

The former occupants of the secret annexe were taken into Silberbauer's office for questioning. Otto Frank was asked if he knew the whereabouts of any other Jews still hiding in Amsterdam. He replied that he did not; having been in hiding himself for two years he had lost touch with everyone. Silberbauer appeared to believe him and did not pursue the matter. The prisoners returned to their cells for the night but were transferred the following day to a regular jail near the center of

Amsterdam. Inside this huge building, dark rooms were filled with row upon row of bunk beds and buckets in the corners to serve as toilets. All night long people cried and shouted and babies wailed. The Franks, the van Pelses and Pfeffer remained there for two days.

On August 8 (four days after their arrest), the Franks and their friends were taken to the central railway station in Amsterdam. The train that arrived to take them out of the city looked like an ordinary one, but as soon as the passengers climbed aboard, the doors were locked and bolted behind them. Despite this, they were hopeful for the future, since by now it was clear that the Germans were losing the war. Anne stayed by the window throughout the train journey, spellbound by the countryside. For a while, it was almost like freedom, but by late afternoon the train had reached its destination: Westerbork.

Surrounded by flat, empty grassland, Westerbork was a miserable place where Jews were held before being sent on to concentration camps. It was encircled by high barbed-wire fences, and armed guards stood in the watchtowers overlooking the compound. More than a hundred wooden barracks, containing rows of three-tier bunks, housed 30,000 people at a time. In the middle of the camp was a railway line, and every Tuesday a train rolled out filled with prisoners bound for the concentration camps of eastern Europe.

The Franks and their friends arrived in Westerbork on the afternoon of August 8 and followed the usual routine for newcomers. They were taken across to the registration desks in the main square, where they handed over their ration cards and gave their personal details to the clerks. Then they were thoroughly searched and asked whether they had any valuables. Finally, they were taken to their barracks and told that they were "Convict Jews" because they had committed the "crime" of going into hiding. This meant that they had even less freedom than the other camp inmates. The men had their heads shaved and the women had their hair cut very short. They were not allowed soap and they received hardly any food. Each day began with roll call, when all the prisoners were checked for attendance by name. At 5 A.M. everyone started work—taking apart old airplane batteries at long tables. They were allowed to talk, but guards stood over them and shouted for them to speed up. At lunchtime they were given a piece of stale bread and a few spoonfuls of watery soup.

Prisoners in Westerbork relied on their friends and family to keep their spirits up. Janny and Lientje Brilleslijper, two Dutch sisters who were also in the punishment section, worked alongside the Frank family. Lientje remembered, "Anne and Margot were very attached to their mother. Anne wrote in the diary that her mother didn't understand her, but I think that was just an adolescent mood. She clung to her mother in the camp."[1]

On the evening of September 2, a German official entered the punishment barracks and began reading from a list. Those inmates whose names were read out were told that they were being deported by train the next morning. Among them were the van Pelses, Pfeffer, and the Franks. Panic broke out immediately. People rushed about, throwing the few belongings they had left into bags, marking their names on the blankets they would be taking with them, and repeating addresses where they could meet after the war, in case they were separated.

At 7 A.M. the next morning, men, women, and children began filing out of the barracks. Each passenger carried a bag over one shoulder and a rolled-up blanket attached to the other with string. The sick and disabled were guided through on stretchers and carts. It took a long time to fill all the carriages, but

---

[1] Brilleslijper-Jaldati, Lientje, in Anderson, Edith, *A Sequel to Anne Frank's Diary*, press clipping, 1966.

at 11 A.M., the whistle blew and the train pulled away, gathering speed as it moved out of the camp and into the unknown.

For three days, the train rumbled through war-torn Europe. People crouched, lay, or stood on the straw-scattered floor of the crowded, rocking carriages. In each carriage, a tiny square window and a hanging lantern gave a little light. A small bucket was filled with drinking water and a larger bucket served as a toilet. Whenever the train stopped, a guard would open the door and throw in some bread. The Franks and their friends sat together on their knapsacks, pressed against the walls. They shared their carriage with the seriously ill in a space that was cramped and cold. Anne, Margot, and Peter talked quietly and occasionally climbed up on the bars to peep out of the window, but they could see nothing.

On the third night, the train started to slow down and finally stopped in front of a long, low building with an arched entrance and a high pointed roof. A loud banging began on the doors, and then there were shouts: "Jews, out, quick OUT!" They had arrived in Auschwitz, the most feared of all concentration camps.

Anne Frank's first impression of Auschwitz was the same as everyone else's aboard the train: glaring searchlights and uniformed male prisoners running along the platform. The men were *Kapos* (Head Prisoners), who reached in and pulled those nearest to them down to the ground. They yelled at the newcomers to hurry. There were shouts and screams as relatives disappeared from view. Above the hissing steam of the cooling train, a loudspeaker ordered: "Women to the left! Men to the right!" Anne watched her father, Hermann van Pels, Peter van Pels, Fritz Pfeffer, and all the other male passengers being herded away by SS guards. It was the last time Anne ever saw her beloved father.

Large trucks took away the elderly and the very young; none of these people were ever seen again. The remaining women were forced to march quickly toward their part of the camp. They were led into a narrow building, where they had their heads shaved. They were given shoes and a gray sack to wear, then shown to a row of desks, where their arms were tattooed with their prison number. Then they were sent to their barracks. Anne, Margot, and Mrs. Frank were placed in Block 29. The buildings were similar to those in Westerbork but dirtier and freezing cold.

At 3:30 A.M. every day in Auschwitz a whistle blew to call out the female inmates. There was always a mad rush to the toilet huts at the back of the camp. Breakfast followed, a brown liquid slopped into one's bowl. Bowls could not be replaced if they were lost, other than through "organizing," the term given to swapping or stealing items (Anne was soon seen wearing a pair of men's long white underpants; she had "organized" them from another woman). Then there was roll call. Women had to stand in a large open square in rows of five to be counted. They were forced to stand in all weathers, often for hours at a time, while punishments were carried out. An eyewitness remembers that Anne and Margot always stood together during roll call, and that Anne was very calm and withdrawn. The march to work took half an hour from Anne's block. Their job was to dig up an area of grass and throw it on top of more grass. The *Kapos* ran among them constantly, screaming, "Faster! Faster!" and beating those who disobeyed. At 12:30 P.M., huge vats of soup were carried into the field. Each woman held out her bowl and received one ladle's worth of green fluid. For half an hour they sat in groups of five, drinking from their bowls, and then they returned to another five hours of digging. At 6 P.M. they marched back to the camp. Their evening meal was a slice of bread and a tiny piece of margarine. The block leader's assistants handed out the bread; Anne was one of them. At 9 P.M. the whistles blew and they were allowed into the barracks to sleep.

On October 27, there was a selection from Anne's block for the youngest and strongest to leave Auschwitz to work in a weapons factory. Everyone desperately wanted to be chosen, knowing that they would have a far greater chance of surviving elsewhere. Anne was rejected because she had scabies (itchy red and black sores caused by lice), and her mother and Margot would not even think about leaving her alone in the camp. She was sent to the Scabies Barrack, and Margot volunteered to join her there. Their mother and a woman they had known in Westerbork dug a hole under the barracks so that they could pass the girls bread and speak to them. After a while, Margot also caught scabies. She and Anne remained in the barracks together. A friend of theirs passed on a watch she had found to Mrs. Frank, who exchanged it with another woman for a loaf of bread, some cheese, and a piece of sausage. Margot and Anne needed the food badly because their health was getting worse every day.

Then, on October 30, another selection took place in Auschwitz. The women were made to stand outside in the icy air for twenty-four hours before being marched into a big hall, where the selection took place. Beside a huge spotlight, Josef Mengele, a Nazi doctor feared by all prisoners because of his cruelty, waited impatiently to decide who would die in the gas chambers and who would be sent to another camp. Although Anne and Margot were still in a terrible condition from the scabies, they were both young, so Mengele ordered them to be sent to another camp. Anne and Margot never saw their mother again.

Without her daughters, Edith Frank lost the will to live. She died of hunger and distress in Auschwitz in January 1945.

Six hundred thirty-four women were selected for the transport to Bergen-Belsen concentration camp. Anne and Margot Frank were among them. They were given old clothing, odd shoes, a blanket, some bread and sausage, and a piece of margarine. Then they were all herded out to the train. No one knew then where they were going, but the journey was appalling. It was bitterly cold and cramped in the wagons, and they received no more food or water. After four days, the train stopped and the SS guards unbolted the doors.

At first, Anne and Margot were housed in a tent with many other women. Inside, it stank and was boiling hot from all the people squashed in together. There were no lights and no toilets. Then the two girls were moved on to a stone hut. They had to share a wooden bunk, and there was only one washroom for thousands of people.

Anne and Margot were given a bunk below Lientje and Janny, their friends from the Westerbork camp two months before. At night, Anne would tell stories and jokes, trying to keep their spirits up. Lientje remembered, "Mostly they were about food. Once we talked about going to the American Hotel in Amsterdam for dinner, and Anne suddenly burst into tears at the thought that we would never get back."[2] They were put to work in the shoe shed, unstitching old shoes by hand. The work was difficult and painful, made worse by the beatings they received from the SS. Anne's hands began to bleed and fester, as did Lientje's, and the two of them had to give up work. They were only able to survive and help others by stealing or begging food from the stores.

At the end of November, Mrs. van Pels arrived in the Belsen camp from Auschwitz. Anne and Margot had not seen her since the journey from Westerbork two months before. She joined their small group immediately. Conditions in the camp became worse when a new commandant was appointed, bringing with him his

---

[2] Brilleslijper-Jaldati, Lientje, "Memories of Anne Frank," in press leaflet for the film *Ein Tagebuch für Anne Frank* (Berlin: VEB Progress film-Vertrieb, 1959).

cruelest staff and taking from the prisoners the few pieces of food they were allowed.

In the middle of this, Anne and her friends tried to celebrate Hanukkah and Christmas. They had managed to save some scraps to eat and gathered together to share what they had. They talked and sang songs. Lientje recalled: "Anne's eyes glittered. She told us more stories. We thought they must be old stories which we did not happen to know. But now I know that they were stories that Anne had made up herself."[3]

In the first days of 1945, prisoners who had been marched from other camps began to arrive in Belsen. Anne tried to find out if there was anyone she knew among them. In February, she met her best friend from Amsterdam, Lies Goslar. It was Mrs. van Pels who brought Anne the news that Lies was in Belsen and looking for her. Anne rushed straight over to the barbed-wire fence separating her part of the camp from Lies's. The two girls cried when they saw each other. Lies told Anne that her mother had died and that she had been sent to Belsen with her father and younger sister. Her father was seriously ill. Anne in turn explained that they

[3] Brilleslijper-Jaldati, Lientje, "Memories of Anne Frank," in press leaflet for the film *Ein Tagebuch für Anne Frank* (Berlin: VEB Progress film-Vertrieb, 1959).

had never gone to Switzerland but had been in hiding in Amsterdam. She said that she believed her mother and father were dead. They talked about the past two years, and Anne told Lies about the gas chambers in Auschwitz. Then she said that she had nothing to eat. Lies still received Red Cross parcels in her barracks, and she promised Anne she would try to help her.

They met again the following night. Lies had packed a woollen jacket, biscuits, sugar, and a tin of sardines for her friend. She threw the bundle over, but when it landed, she remembered, "I heard an agonized cry from Anne. When I asked what was the matter, she said another woman had caught the bundle and wouldn't give it up."[4] The next evening, Lies threw over another package, and this time Anne caught it, but after that the two friends had no more contact. Lies's father died, and soon after Lies herself became sick.

As winter took hold, Margot also fell ill. She had dysentery, an extreme form of diarrhea, which left her exhausted and unable to stand. She and Anne were sent to the sick barracks, which were slightly warmer than the rest but filled with infectious prisoners. Lientje and

---

[4] Pick-Goslar, Hanneli, in Yaroch, Patricia, "Her Best Friend Reveals a Surprising New Side of the Little Girl Whose Diary Touched the Heart of the World," 1957.

Janny visited them there. Margot could not speak. There was no water and no food, other than what Lientje and Janny were able to give them. Everywhere around them, people were dying of starvation and typhus. Eventually, Margot and Anne were sent back to their old barracks, despite being severely ill themselves. They slept on the bunk beside the door, where drafts came stinging through, night and day. Survivors remember them always screaming, "Close the door, close the door!" Both girls showed all the symptoms of typhus: high fever, severe pain, skin rashes, and delirium. When Lientje saw them again, she knew that they were in the last stages of the disease. She remembered, "Margot had fallen from the bunk and was half unconscious. Anne was already very feverish. She was very friendly and loving. 'Margot will sleep well and when she sleeps I don't need to get up anymore.'"[5] Margot was too weak to survive the fall onto the cold stone floor. The shock killed her.

Anne now gave in to the typhus raging through her own small body. She was so filled with horror at the thought of all the lice on her that she threw away her clothes and walked about, when she was able, in only a

---

[5] Brilleslijper-Jaldati, Lientje, "Memories of Anne Frank," in press leaflet for the film *Ein Tagebuch für Anne Frank* (Berlin: VEB Progress Film-Vertrieb 1959).

thin blanket. Janny and Lientje gave her some bread and tried to find clothing for her, but the end was very near for Anne. The death of Margot was more than she could stand. She thought she had nothing to live for. In March 1945, Anne died in Belsen, alone.

On April 15, 1945, only two or three weeks after the death of Anne Frank, British troops arrived and freed the remaining prisoners in Belsen.

Chapter Six:
The Diary

"I want to publish a book entitled *Het Achterhuis*
after the war. ..."
(*Anne Frank's Diary*, May 11, 1944)

Of the eight people who hid in the secret annexe, Anne's
father, Otto Frank, was the only one who survived. He
was still in Auschwitz when it was liberated. The Russian
soldiers who set all the surviving prisoners free handed
out clothing and food, and separated those who were
dying from those who might live. Mr. Frank was given a
bunk of his own in a different barracks. He immediately
began asking people if they knew what had happened to
his wife and daughters. He found out that his wife was
dead. From that moment on, Mr. Frank put all his efforts
and hope into the belief that his daughters were still
alive. Throughout his long journey by train and boat
back to Amsterdam, he asked everyone he saw about
Margot and Anne, but no one had any news.

Mr. Frank arrived in Amsterdam on June 3, 1945. He

went straight to Miep and Jan's apartment, having no home of his own to which he could return. His friends were overwhelmed with joy to see him and said he could stay with them as long as he wished. He told them that Edith was dead but that he was sure Margot and Anne were still alive. Miep and Jan were also convinced that the two girls would return. Miep was so certain of this that she did not tell Mr. Frank about the object she kept in her desk at work: Anne's diary.

She had found it on the day of the arrest. After the Gestapo had left the building, she, Jan, and Bep had gone to the annexe to see what damage had been done. Everything was in a complete mess, with drawers pulled open and objects scattered around. The floor was buried under piles of books and papers. Looking more closely, Miep realized that many of the papers belonged to Anne. She pointed out the diary to Bep, who picked it up. Quickly, the two women sorted through the jumble for anything bearing Anne's handwriting. They also saved a photograph album, schoolbooks, reading books, Anne's shoe bag embroidered with her initials, and a little book of quotations compiled by Anne. Returning to the office, Miep placed the diary in her desk, determined to keep it under lock and key until she could hand it back to Anne. The diary was her private property, Miep felt, and for this reason she said nothing to Mr. Frank about having found it.

Immediately following his arrival in Amsterdam, Mr. Frank went back to his old job at the Prinsengracht office. He was delighted to find Kugler and Kleiman there as well. Both had survived imprisonment in Dutch camps. While they had been in prison, Miep had taken charge of the business, but now everyone stepped back into his or her old job. There was one difference in the warehouse, however. One of the warehousemen, called van Maaren, whom Mr. Frank and his helpers suspected had betrayed them, had been dismissed after he was caught stealing from the inventory. They were all relieved to see him go.

When Mr. Frank wasn't working, he spent every spare minute questioning people, checking survivor lists, calling the Red Cross organization, and placing advertisements in the press, all in the hope of finding his daughters. In July he received news at last, but it was not the news he had longed to hear. Visiting the Red Cross, he had seen a list with "x's" placed beside the names of those who had not survived. Anne and Margot Frank were listed—and crossed off. The woman who had made the marks was Janny Brilleslijper, who, together with her sister, Lientje, had been among the last to see Anne and

Margot. Mr. Frank visited Janny at home shortly afterward, needing to hear the news directly from her. Janny told him helplessly, "Your daughters are . . . no more." She watched in horror as he went white and fell into a chair, his last shred of hope taken from him.

When Miep heard the news, her first thoughts—other than those of deep sorrow—were of Anne's diary. She knew she now had to give it to Mr. Frank. At the time, he was sitting alone in his office with his head in his hands. She placed the papers on his desk and said softly, "Here is your daughter Anne's legacy to you." On top of the pile lay the red-checked diary. Miep left the room, and Mr. Frank opened the book, its pages untouched since Anne herself had last written in it. And there she was, on the first page, smiling up at him from a school photograph. Mr. Frank began to read: *Gorgeous photograph, isn't it!!! . . . On Friday, 12th June, I woke up at six o'clock and no wonder; it was my birthday . . .*

With the knowledge that both his children were dead, Mr. Frank turned his efforts to finding people he had known before the war. He already knew that his friends who had hidden with him in the secret annexe had all died in different camps, and he discovered that few others had survived. However, Anne's friends Lies Goslar and Jacqueline van Maarsen were still alive, and he visited them often. He also wrote to his own family in Switzerland, and in one letter he mentioned Anne's diary for the first time: ". . . I don't have photos from the last years of course, but Miep by chance saved an album and Anne's diary. But I didn't have the strength to read it all. . . ."[1]

Soon though, Mr. Frank did begin to read the diary, and he found it difficult to put down. In his memoir, written many years later, he explained how he felt about it: "I began to read slowly, only a few pages each day, more would have been impossible, as I was overwhelmed by painful memories. For me, it was a revelation. There, was revealed a completely different Anne to the child that I had lost. I had no idea of the depth of her thoughts and feelings. . . . Through Anne's accurate description of every event and every person, all the details of being in hiding become clear to me again."[2]

Mr. Frank copied out the diary for his mother and sister in Switzerland, using a combination of Anne's original diary and the version she rewrote with a view to publication. He left out the parts he thought were less interesting and those entries where Anne had written

---

[1] Frank, Otto, letter, undated. Private collection of Buddy Elias.
[2] Frank, Otto, memoir. Private collection of Buddy Elias.

most angrily about her mother. He asked a friend to help him translate Anne's words from Dutch into German, because his mother knew no Dutch. Mr. Frank mailed the whole thing bit by bit to his mother. His family in Switzerland was astounded by it, as was his friend, Werner Cahn, who told him he felt it should be published. Mr. Frank thought for a long time about this and in the end decided that it was what Anne would have wanted. In his memoir he wrote: "Anne would have so much loved to see something published. . . . Initially, I was very reluctant to publish, but then again and again I saw that my friends were right. . . . The first edition of the diary appeared in 1947. Anne would have been so proud."[3]

The first Dutch edition, published in June 1947, sold out after six months, and a second edition was printed to meet demand. Mr. Frank then sent the manuscript to publishers in Germany, who were reluctant to publish it at first, feeling it might stir up a lot of bad feelings among the German people, but when it appeared in Germany in 1950 it sold well. The diary was published in France that same year, where it was a success, and appeared in Britain and the United States two years later. In America

---

[3] Frank, Otto, memoir. Private collection of Buddy Elias.

it became an instant best-seller, but it took rather longer for the British public to appreciate it. The diary was published in Japan in 1952 and, again, sold well immediately.

By the mid 1950s, Otto Frank was spending several hours a day answering the letters he received from people who had read the diary. So popular had Anne's words become that in 1955 a play based on the diary opened in New York. It was highly successful and won many awards, going on to tour throughout Europe. More than 1 million people saw the play in Germany, and sales of the diary soared. Youth groups there were established in Anne's name, schools and streets were named after her, a group of two thousand teenagers traveled to Bergen-Belsen to commemorate her death, and at her former home in Frankfurt a plaque was attached to the wall. In 1957, a film of the diary was made, which brought Anne Frank's words to yet more people.

Ever since the earliest publication of the diary, people had been knocking on the door of 263 Prinsengracht to ask if they could look around the secret annexe, and on May 4, 1960, it officially opened as a museum called the Anne Frank House. Several changes were made to the front house, where the offices and warehouse had been, but the annexe was kept as near as possible to how it had looked when Anne had been in hiding there. Mr. Frank insisted that the annexe should remain empty, however; that was how it had been left after the arrest, when the Nazis took away all their furniture. After retiring from his businesses, Mr. Frank and his second wife, Fritzi Geiringer (who had been a neighbor of the Franks before the war), moved to Switzerland. Fritzi helped her husband with the vast amount of correspondence generated by Anne's diary, which he had taken with him to Switzerland. Today, the Anne Frank House receives more than 800,000 visitors a year.

For the rest of his life, Otto Frank had to deal with extremists—people who said that his daughter's diary was a fake, written by someone else after the war to make money. Recently the diary has undergone a series of scientific tests which have proved, beyond doubt, that it is a real document written by Anne Frank, no one else. Mr. Frank was in good health until the last year of his life, when he became ill. He died on August 19, 1980, at home in Switzerland. He was ninety-one years old.

Today Miep Gies is the sole surviving member of the five "helpers." Before their deaths, they were all given the highest honor possible to those who helped the Jews during wartime: each was awarded the accolade of "the

Righteous of the Nations" by Yad Vashem, the Holocaust Memorial Center in Israel.

One thing has always intrigued readers of the diary over the years: who told the Nazis about the occupants of the secret annexe? There have been two official investigations into the matter, but neither has come up with a definite answer. In 1945, Kleiman went to the authorities with a letter in which he made it clear that he, and the other helpers, strongly suspected the warehouseman, van Maaren, had called the Gestapo. They knew that throughout the war he had been stealing from them, and Kugler also once caught him scraping the blue paint from the windows overlooking the annexe and muttering, "Well, I've never been over there." He set traps in the warehouse at night: pencils laid on the very edge of a desk, where any movement would dislodge them, and potato flour dropped on the floor to show footprints. When he was asked about this behavior, he said, quite reasonably, that he was merely trying to catch the real thief to prove he was not to blame. Yet the occupants of the secret annexe were frightened of him, and Anne wrote several times in her diary that she was worried he would give them away. But there was never any proof that van Maaren had betrayed them. We will probably never know who did.

Anne's diary is now in Amsterdam once again, on display in the secret annexe. It has become a phenomenon, and Anne herself is now a historical figure. There are Anne Frank roses and tulips, statues, stamps, medals, and awards; an Anne Frank Day is observed annually on June 12, and exhibitions are held throughout the world. A forest of 10,000 trees grows in her honor in Israel, and a waxwork of her sits in Amsterdam's Madame Tussaud's, yet behind all this is a very ordinary girl. Many thousands of words have been written about her and the power of her diary, but perhaps the last word on the subject should go to her father, Otto Frank, who did so much to ensure that his daughter would never be forgotten: "I once asked my publisher what, in his opinion, are the reasons why the diary has been read by so many. He said that each reader can find something that moves him personally. And that seems to be right. . . . Parents and teachers learn from it, how difficult it is to really know their children or their pupils. . . . Young people identify with Anne or see in her a friend. 'I want to live on after my death' Anne wrote, and you could well say that her wish has come true, because she lives on in the hearts of so many people."[4]

---

[4] Frank, Otto, memoir. Private collection of Buddy Elias.

Glossary

Anti-Semitism: Hatred of Jewish people. For centuries, anti-Semitism has existed and has often resulted in Jews being forced to leave their homes, beaten, and murdered. Six million Jews were murdered in the Holocaust—an example of where anti-Semitism and persecution can lead.

Auschwitz: The world's largest death camp, where approximately 4 million people (2 million of them Jews) were murdered.

Barracks/Block: Barnlike building in which concentration camp inmates lived and slept in horrific conditions.

Bergen-Belsen: Concentration camp in northern Germany. Here, there were no gas chambers and prisoners were not always forced to work, but thousands died from starvation and disease.

Concentration camps: Centers used to imprison Jews, political opponents of the Nazis, and minority groups under terrible conditions. People died of starvation, misery, disease, and hard labor. Some of the camps, known as extermination, or death, camps, were also built with gas chambers and crematoriums in which whole families were murdered.

Deportation: The organized removal of Jews from the countries in which they lived to the concentration camps.

Gestapo: The German Secret State Police, who were responsible for enforcing laws and preventing opposition to Hitler.

Ghetto: Fenced-off area of a European city in which Jews were made to live in extreme poverty and where the threat of death was always present.

Hanukkah: A Jewish festival that celebrates the victory of the Jews against Syrian persecution. Known as "The Festival of Lights," it also commemorates the miracle that occurred when the Jews came to rededicate the Temple and found that although they had only enough oil to light the lamp for one single day, it lasted for eight.

Invasion: Entry into a land by an army from another country with the aim of taking over. On May 10, 1940, the German army invaded the Netherlands.

Kapo: A head prisoner in a concentration camp. The Kapos were well known for their cruelty.

Kristallnacht: "Night of the Broken Glass." Name given to events of

November 9–10, 1938, during which Jews were beaten and deported, their homes and businesses were ruined, and synagogues throughout Germany and Austria were destroyed.

Liberal Jews: People of the Jewish religion who are not devout followers of the Jewish laws.

Liberation: The freeing of prisoners from concentration camps. Many were so ill and mistreated that they died not long after they were liberated.

Nazis/National Socialists: German political party that promoted nationalism, racism, and dictatorship; set up in 1920, it was soon led by Adolf Hitler and was voted into power in 1933.

Occupation: The control of one country by another country, usually through miliary force. Following the invasion of May 10, 1940, Germany occupied the Netherlands.

Organizing: Camp slang for exchanging one thing for another. A pair of shoes might be traded for a few slices of bread; so the bread had been "organized" by the prisoner.

Passover: Jewish religious festival that commemorates the Israelites' exodus from slavery in Egypt.

Rationing: The limiting of food and other supplies to a certain amount per person. Coupons are given to everyone to ensure that only a set amount of goods can be bought.

Refugees: People who leave one country for another after being persecuted and look for somewhere safe to live.

Reichstag: Headquarters of the German government.

Resistance: Organized groups of people actively opposed to the Nazi government. Many Jews in hiding relied on the Resistance for their "homes" and their survival.

Sabbath: The most important ritual in Judaism. The Jewish Sabbath commences at sundown on Friday night with the lighting of candles and ends at sunset the following day. It is a day of rest and spiritual enrichment.

SS: Powerful Nazi military organization, Hitler's protection unit, which murdered his "enemies" wherever they went. The guards in the concentration camps were members of the SS.

Swastika: A very old religious symbol that Hitler used as the emblem of the Nazi Party.

Synagogue: Building in which Jews come together to pray, celebrate religious festivals, and worship God.

Typhus: Agonizing infectious disease, passed from one person to another. It killed thousands in the camps, including Margot and Anne Frank.

Westerbork: Camp in the northern Netherlands, where Jews were held until deportation to Auschwitz and other concentration camps.

The Yellow Star: Six-pointed yellow star that Jews were made to wear as a badge in the occupied countries to mark them out for humiliation and deportation.

About the Author

Carol Ann Lee was born in Yorkshire, England, in 1969. She began work on a biography of Anne Frank when she was just eighteen years old, but she put it aside while she went to college. At Manchester University she studied the history of art and design.

Her interest in Anne sparked an interest in the Holocaust, and she interviewed many Holocaust survivors to learn about their experiences.

It wasn't until 1998 that she completed *Roses from the Earth: The Biography of Anne Frank*. It was published by Viking Books to substantial critical and public acclaim. It has so far appeared in thirteen languages. *Anne Frank's Story* is her second book. Carol Ann Lee is married and has a baby son. She lives in Amsterdam, where she is working on her next book: the first full-length biography of Otto Frank.